Contents

Giving Confident Presentations

Rowmark

Other Easy Step by Step Guides in the series include:

Successful Selling

Marketing

Stress and Time Management

Motivating your Staff

Recruiting the Right Staff

Better Budgeting for your Business

Building a Positive Media Profile

Writing Advertising Copy

Writing Articles and Newsletters

Managing Change

Telemarketing, Cold Calling and Appointment Making

Handling Confrontation

All the above guides are available direct from:

Rowmark Limited
Unit 36
Broadmarsh Business & Innovation Centre
Harts Farm Way
Havant
Hampshire PO9 1HS
Telephone: 023 9244 9665
Fax: 023 9244 9601

Email: enquiries@rowmark.co.uk

Or via our web site www.rowmark.co.uk

Easy Step by Step Guide

Giving Confident Presentations

Brian Lomas

Rowmark

Published by Rowmark Limited
Unit 36 Broadmarsh Innovation Centre
Havant
Hampshire
PO9 1HS

First published in 2002
ISBN 0–9539856–7–9

Typeset by Freelance Publishing Services, Brinscall, Lancs
www.freelancepublishingservices.co.uk
Printed in Great Britain by RPM Reprographics Ltd, Chichester

About the author

Brian Lomas is a business consultant and trainer based on the south coast of England. He is a visiting lecturer at the Southampton University School of Management and has written the Easy Step by Step Guide, *Stress and Time Management*, also published by Rowmark.

His first experience of public speaking was as a 5-year old sitting on his father's knee and talking into a megaphone. What did he say? Four words: 'Vote for my daddy.'

Although his dad didn't get elected to the House of Commons on that occasion, neither Lomas gave up their public speaking. Lomas the Elder did become a Member of Parliament and Brian watched, listened, practiced and learnt during a business career on both sides of the Atlantic.

And has he learnt? Well, his dad thought so and he didn't offer praise easily. On his parents golden wedding anniversary (when Brian was somewhat older than five), his dad took him to one side after he had made his speech and said: 'Well, Brian, how did I do?'

During his career, Brian has presented to audiences in excess of a thousand, faced the friendly (and the not-so-friendly), been asked the questions he wanted and the questions he didn't want. And when asked: 'Are you nervous when presenting?', Brian answered, 'Absolutely! In fact, the more laid-back I might feel, the more dangerous it is. Nerves make for a good presentation – the trick is to appear and speak confidently. And that trick – along with many others – is what this book is all about.'

Acknowledgements

The author would like to acknowledge the help, support and editorial comments by Mark Adams and Pauline Rowson in compiling this book. Thank you.

Dedicated to my dad – he made it all look so easy!

Introduction

As a trainer, consultant, compère, after-dinner speaker and lay-politician, I have presented to a wide range of audiences and on a vast array of subjects. By adding this experience to that of others and by observing other presenters, this easy step by step guide brings together the knowledge, skills, experience and attitudes necessary to deliver a confident presentation.

Presenting and **public speaking** are treated alike in this guide, since many of the principles for one apply equally to the other.

For some of you, presenting may be one of your greatest fears, perhaps ranking alongside going to the dentist (no offence to any of that profession) or being put in a cage with a hungry lion (or two). Wherever a presentation sits along the 'fear-scale' for you, this guide is designed to help you, if not actually to the point of enjoying it.

Yet you might enjoy presenting and have done for years. So how will this guide help you? Well, ask yourself whether or not there is anything left for you to learn about how you prepare, rehearse and then deliver a presentation. If there is, read on!

How to use this guide

You can take it step by step beginning with preparation then rehearsal and delivery. Even better, before starting a new chapter, apply what you have learnt to a forthcoming (or imaginary) presentation you have to make.

Alternatively, the terminology and techniques in the first two chapters are referred to subsequently – so I strongly recommend that you read them first. You could then look in the index for your specific area of interest and jump straight to it.

If you want to dip in and out of this guide, you will see within each chapter some text that is 'boxed' which highlight key tips to help you. And at the end of each chapter is a useful summary of the points covered, so you can pick which chapters would initially add the most value.

Finally, a cautionary note. This guide seeks to give you a lot to think about – don't try to do everything on your first attempt. Your brain simply won't cope! The path to successful presenting is exactly that – a path that you must take, learning something new as you go, and moving on only when each new idea has become second nature, a subconscious activity.

What you will learn from this guide

- how to approach the whole issue of giving presentations and break it down into manageable chunks

- the importance of defining exactly what your presentation should achieve

- what you must research and prepare for in advance

- how to manage information overload

- different ways to structure a presentation

- effective use of scripts, prompts, visual aids and handouts

- handling questions – including the awkward ones!

- how to present yourself – your voice, body language and appearance

- the importance of self-belief.

1

Different types of message

A presentation is a transmission of a message.

Preparing a presentation starts with identifying the type of message to be transmitted and how the presenter will know that the message has been received and, most importantly, understood.

There are three types of message:

- **To transfer information**
  this could be training, teaching, lecturing or, without perhaps such formality of purpose, to simply inform the audience about something

- **To contribute to a discussion**
  whether simply seeking others' opinions or the presenters conveying their own. Such a presentation may, or may not, seek to reach a specific conclusion

- **To create a reaction**
  Perhaps laughter. Or it could be to tell or persuade

the audience to do something specific. For instance – staff might be told to adopt new working practices (although persuasion would deliver better long-term results) or you might persuade or influence someone to buy your products or services.

> You must determine the type of message you want to transmit.
>
> Is it *to transfer information, contribute to a discussion* or *create a reaction?*

There may be occasions when you want to transmit more than just one type of message. For instance, you need to explain the range of your services for sale and thereby initiate a discussion. Following that discussion, you want to sell those services that meet the purchasers' needs. You may even want to entertain your would-be buyers as you speak.

That's fine – perhaps a little ambitious, but it can work. However:

> It is vital to determine the overriding message – what is the *end result* you seek to achieve?

In this example, your aim is to create a reaction – that is, to persuade the audience to buy your services.

Is a presentation the right medium?

A presentation is but one way to communicate. Having determined the type of message you want to convey, ask yourself whether or not a presentation is the best way to achieve success.

There are no hard and fast rules here, but as a guide:

- if you seek to persuade or influence others to act, your likelihood of success will be higher with face-to-face communication

- the greater the likelihood of the audience wanting to ask you questions, the greater the need for face-to-face communication

- if you have an audience of one or two, a presentation is likely to be perceived as too formal or controlling

- if you have masses of information to transmit, the audience is likely to suffer 'information overload' during a presentation and fail to grasp the key points. (However, this scenario may still suit a presentation if handouts are distributed – see Chapter 6)

- consider whether or not a presentation will be perceived by your audience as worthwhile. (No one appreciates travelling 200 miles for a 15-minute presentation that could have been summed up in an email).

> Check before proceeding further:
> is a presentation the right medium to achieve
> your end result?

Defining the primary aim

Now we need to refine our type of message in to something more specific. This is called the **primary aim**.

First, let's consider the possible consequences of *not* developing our message type further.

Let's say that my boss asks me to deliver a presentation to initiate a discussion on our new products with an important customer. I make a superb presentation (from my perspective) about all the benefits, quality and value the products offer. During the discussion that follows, the audience complains about the poor quality of the new products that they have already bought.

I should have noticed the resistance to my message during the presentation – perhaps there was negative body language. But even then, it would have been too late. If I had refined the type of message during my preparation, I could have saved myself from embarrassment and probable failure. So our refined message could include:

- that the customer explains before the discussion ends all the known quality issues with the new product range

- that the customer agrees they will buy each of the products again, within three months of resolving the quality issues

- that in the following twelve months, the purchases by this customer of our new products increase by at least 10 per cent.

Coupled with perhaps a willingness to shake my hand at the end of the presentation and a diary commitment to meet again within the month, I now have a complete primary aim. I will be able to measure how the presentation has gone both at the end of the presentation and over the coming months.

We achieved this by asking the following questions:

> What am I seeking to achieve?
>
> Why is this presentation being made?
>
> How would I recognise success?

What am I seeking to achieve?
Example answers could include:

- to sell products/services

- to train computer skills

- to entertain the audience

- to solicit ideas for improving quality.

Now, refine this further by asking ...

Why is this presentation being made?
This question should give us the information to build a realistic and measurable **primary aim**. To continue with our examples:

To sell products/ services ...	the potential customer has never bought from us and this is the best way to introduce an extensive range
To train computer skills ...	there is a need to train each staff member to start using new software
To entertain the audience ...	the audience want some light relief after a hard day
To solicit ideas for improving quality ...	management do not have all the answers – they need input from everyone

There may be much more information generated than that shown in the examples above.

Now we can ask our third question.

How would I recognise success?
This is critical. There are many ways that a presentation could be judged a success. For instance:

- it ends with a round of applause

- the audience asks at least six questions

- no-one leaves the handouts behind

- no-one falls asleep while you are speaking

And most importantly:

- your primary aim is achieved.

So why bother trying to identify multiple success criteria? Well, if you only have one measure of success – perhaps the round of applause – and you don't get that applause, your presentation has failed to achieve your aim. Worse still, you might feel a failure too.

If you have multiple criteria, you really should avoid abject failure. (Putting it another way, you would have to do absolutely everything wrong!). However, if you have five criteria and do not achieve one of them, you are still 80 per cent successful.

Multiple criteria will also help you in developing a style and structure for your presentation. To illustrate:

It ends with a round of applause …	you must be upbeat, polished – you may 'plant' someone in the audience to start them off!
The audience ask at least six questions …	you need to give the audience opportunity to both think of and ask questions. Giving new information in your answers will encourage more questions
No-one leaves behind the handouts …	handouts will have to be well presented and perhaps expand on some points you raised.
No one falls asleep while you are speaking …	again, be upbeat and the timing will be crucial (don't have a breakfast meeting if everyone is partying the night before!)

Each of the above success criteria could be relevant to most presentations. However, you must also introduce further criteria in respect of your primary aim. Again, with our previous examples, we could start with:

By the end of the presentation …

To sell products/ services …	the customer buys £10,000 of new product
To train computer skills …	everyone operates key functions of their new software without assistance
To entertain the audience …	I have to stop talking at least three times until the audience stops laughing
To solicit ideas for improving quality …	the audience identify 12 new ideas

And there could be further success criteria for **after** the end of the presentation:

To sell products/ services …	the customer buys £100,000 of new products within a year
To train computer skills …	everyone uses the new software at least once a week for the next 6 months
To entertain the audience …	I am re-booked to entertain the same audience within the year
To solicit ideas for improving quality …	the company gets at least 10 ideas per month for the next year

> It is essential to identify *multiple* yet *realistic* success criteria for your primary aim.

Why are you the presenter?

This question is always worth asking. It may give you some positive feedback:

'... you always present so professionally'

'... you know more about it than anyone else'

'... we want you to improve your profile within the organisation'

It could, however, give you new information:

'... you are going to be increasingly involved in this part of the business'

'... we want to see how you react under pressure'

'... the audience specifically asked for you'

Stay focused

Having spent the time developing the primary aim, use it! Everything that now happens in respect of your presentation should be focused to deliver this aim. If something doesn't contribute to it, you must discard it immediately.

> To stay focused, ensure the primary aim remains visible throughout the preparation and rehearsal stages of your presentation.

In summary

- determine the end result of a presentation – is it to transfer information, contribute to a discussion or create a reaction?

- be certain that a presentation is the right communication medium for you

- define the **primary aim** of the presentation

- be specific about what success criteria you seek to reasonably achieve from your presentation

- the more success criteria you identify, the more successful you will be

- identify why the presentation is being made

- know why you are the presenter

- stay focused on your primary aim.

2

Do you need to know it all?

A frequent anxiety of presenters is the question:

> 'Do I need to know it all?
>
> 'The short answer is 'no'.

In fact, I would suggest it's impossible to know everything about your chosen subject. The trick is:

> *Either* know a little more than your audience or acknowledge your audience's expertise and act as a facilitator rather than informer.

Do not 'make up' information. This is particularly true when answering questions (see Chapter 8). It is okay to say 'I don't know' **providing** you promise to find out the answer and get back to the audience within a stated timeframe.

> You must, however, portray confidence in being chosen as the presenter.

Sourcing information

Ensure that you have your primary aim clearly in mind to you when sourcing information. Gather all the relevant information possible – you can sort out later what to use.

There are a multitude of sources available to you – some of the most typical are:

- your own knowledge and experience

- books, publications, the internet, libraries

- professional bodies, (other) experts

- organisations or colleagues who might have relevant experiences, skills or related documents

- the audience themselves (find out examples from them in advance to illustrate your presentation).

> Remember to respect copyright restrictions on any material you use.

Collating data

Before starting your research, think about how you are going to organise/collate it, so when you arrive at a particular point in your preparation, you can find it easily. You could:

- list the various sources and, as you develop your presentation, look up each reference in turn

- copy out everything you discover (remember the rules of copyright!), ideally under key headings

- note key words or phrases to prompt you.

And some people will do it differently. You need to find the way that suits you. Personally, I:

- place my primary aim in front of me

- collate everything that I know about the subject under a series of key headings

- add supplemental notes from my research. I will avoid making judgments about whether or not I agree with the researched material. In fact, contradictory information is a bonus – it will prompt me to think things through for myself

Then:

- I read through all of the file and put it aside

- after a little time (to avoid retyping what I have just read) I develop my presentation

- I will only refer to the research if I get 'stuck'

- when reasonably happy with my preparation, I review the research to see if there is anything obvious that I have missed and check whether I have abused any copyright and, if not, identify any sources I have used

- with perhaps a few later additions, I then develop it into the finished article.

This process works for me because:

- the presentation is a collation of my own thoughts, opinions and words – since I do not have a photographic memory, it isn't a repetition of someone else's

- it allows me to develop a flow through the script without breaking to check references

- it is a unique product and therefore far more likely to interest my audience.

Choosing the information to include

Focus on your primary aim. To achieve it:

- What **must** you talk about?

- What **should** you talk about? (To achieve the aim particularly well)

- What **could** you talk about? (If you felt like it or if you had surplus time)

- What **assumptions** are you making in answering any of the above questions?

An example:

Let's say my **primary** aim is to explain to the audience how to 'wash up the pots' and that one of the **measures** is that they will all be able to wash up as a result.

- I **must** include that they will need pots and water and a description (probably a demonstration) of the interaction between the two. If this, and only this, is remembered, at least everyone will still be able to wash up – even though most of us might not consider it very hygienic

- So what **should** I include to ensure that the washing-up will be done **to a high standard**? I should include the need for clean, hot (but not scalding) water, liquid soap and preferably both a bowl (or equivalent) to wash up in and a means by which the pots can then be rinsed

- And what **could** I add if I wanted? I could mention that some people clean the pots using (clean) sand. Or, to avoid it, you could buy disposable pots or buy a dishwasher!

- And what **assumptions** have I made? Mainly that the audience know what water and pots are! I have also assumed that two hands can be used in the inter-action between pot and water.

Having identified your assumptions, you should check with the audience whether or not they are likely to understand your presentation.

To recap:

> Sort the information into what you *must* include, what you *should* (to do it well) and what you *could* talk about if you wanted.

And then:

> Check what assumptions you have made in sorting this information.

Too little time?

If you have too little time to deliver your entire presentation, deliver only that which you **must** include. Preferably, you will discuss the **shoulds** and, if you have extra time, you can include some of the **coulds**.

If you can't fit the **must** information into the timeframe, you will need to either:

- secure a longer timeframe, or

- reduce the scope of your primary aim.

If you have more than six pieces of information that you **must** include, there is a danger of 'information overload'. Consider distributing some of the information in handouts – see Chapter 6.

In summary

- remember that you don't need to know it all

- use all the information sources available to you in compiling your research

- plan how you intend to collate your research before you start

- choose the information to include in your presentation by asking what must you include to achieve your primary aim, what should you include to excel in meeting your aim and what could you include if you felt like it

- check what assumptions you are making in sorting your information into the three categories. Are your assumptions valid?

- check that you have enough time to communicate the 'must-do' information. If not, reduce the scope of your primary aim or gain more time.

3
Your audience

Before looking at the relationship between the audience and the presenter, we must first check whether or not the aims of the two match.

In Chapter 1, we looked at creating a primary aim. One example I quoted was a 'mismatch' between what the presenter intended (to promote a new product range) and the audience's intention to complain about the poor quality of those products. With the benefit of hindsight, we needed a primary aim that met the needs and expectations of the audience.

> A mismatch of needs or expectations between the presenter and the audience can have disastrous consequences on a presentation.

So how can you ensure that the audience is coming to your presentation with the same purpose in mind?

The easy answer is to ask. So check that their under-standing matches yours **before** you embark further on your preparation. Also:

> Check with the person who asked you to be the presenter:
>
> 'I believe that this is what I should be seeking to achieve ... do you agree?'

The basic information needed

You need to know the size of your audience:

- Who wants to attend?

- Who will be offended if not invited?

- Who will need to attend to achieve your primary aim?

- How many can a pre-determined location accom-modate? (Ideally, the location should be chosen **after** the audience numbers have been agreed).

Your audience – your invite

There are three advantages to inviting your own au-dience:

- you can explain your primary aim in advance (which minimises the likelihood of a mismatch of aims)

- you can ensure everyone is invited who is needed to achieve your primary aim

- you can ensure that those who might seek to hinder your aims **are** there. This may sound a little strange – but it is better to deal with any opposition up front (and when you are likely to have some allies in the audience).

Your audience – invited by others

Even if a third party is the organiser of the invitations, seek to achieve the above points through them.

If you have been unable to publicise your primary aim in advance, it is worth checking with a sample of the audience:

- What have they been told in their invite?

- What do they expect from the presentation?

- What does the organiser expect and need from you?

And finally:

- How well do the answers to the above questions 'match' your primary aim?

Attitudes of the audience

Knowing the attitude of an audience at the start of your presentation can help you to determine the appropriate style, content and structure.

It should also enable you to judge whether or not your primary aim is realistic – the higher the scepticism of your audience, the lower your criteria for success should be. If the audience is highly positive, you should reflect a high expectancy in your primary aim.

So – what makes them feel negative or positive?

People generally feel positive towards your presentation if they believe it will meet their needs and expectations.

A negative attitude might pervade for those who have been 'forced' to attend as well as those who do not understand the relevance of the presentation to them as individuals. Negativity will also arise when people feel pressured to be 'somewhere else' or simply because they 'got out of the wrong side of the bed' that morning.

However:

> Note that whatever the initial attitude of the audience, it can change within seconds of beginning your presentation.

Invitations that work

Encourage your audience to attend – how will they benefit by giving their time to you?

Do ensure that the benefit you offer is relevant – promising a free glass of wine will not motivate everyone (not least those who don't drink!) So there will need to be more than one benefit identified in the invite, so everyone will find **something** in it for themselves.

The more negative their initial attitude to your presentation, the harder you will have to work to convey that benefit effectively.

> **Always explain in an invitation what the audience will personally gain by their attendance.**

Audience knowledge level

Your audience's knowledge level will dictate much of the content, style and language you are going to use during your presentation.

For example, you are to make a presentation on how to make a cake as per your grandmother's recipe. Everyone is going to try it out at home and return the next day with the results.

- if your audience are cooking novices, when you talk of 'folding' the mixture, they will (most probably) fail to understand you. You will need to explain each stage with precision

- however, if your audience members are chefs, you should be able to use cooking jargon relatively freely. The chefs will also seek recognition for their existing knowledge and therefore expect you to explain the recipe relatively quickly.

So always check carefully what the audience actually know but always err on the side of caution.

> **Beware of making assumptions – your audience may not know what you expect them to.**

It is likely that the audience will have mixed levels of knowledge. So to ensure that all the audience will understand (without patronising them), you could:

- single out those who are knowledgeable and explain that you need their attendance for a specific reason. Perhaps they could be there to check you are delivering the right message? Or maybe they can help you in answering difficult questions or give you feedback on your presentation?

- show (without discussion) pre-prepared visual aids that explain jargon. For instance: Verbally one would say 'PC', but on a visual we would show 'PC (political correctness)'

- explain jargon with a smile. For instance, 'Just in case you were wondering if you are in the right presentation, the abbreviation "PC" in this presentation refers not to personal computers but rather political correctness'

- distribute a glossary of terms before you start speaking. (It will only be read by those who need it).

> Your goal should be to ensure that the person with the least knowledge has the opportunity to gain total understanding.

Stereotyping your audience

The more you know about your audience, the easier it will be to tailor your presentation to meet their expectations and needs.

At risk of being politically ***incorrect***, the style (if not content) of a presentation could be different according to the profile of the audience.

Consider ***whether*** *or* ***not***:

- you would change the language in a presentation for teenagers from that used for senior citizens

- you would choose a different perspective when presenting on, for instance, urban regeneration to one group from a depressed part of the country and another from an affluent part

- you would choose different illustrations when discussing, for instance, ethics, to two groups of opposing moral views.

There is no easy answer here. It may be politically incorrect to treat people differently and yet in certain circumstances you may fail in your primary aim if you treat them all the same. And to decide whether or not to treat audiences differently, we are presupposing that you can find out the profile of the audience in a politically correct (and legal) way.

So what might be politically incorrect? Well, any stereotyping of a group of people by nature of their age, gender, race or belief system.

What's the best thing to do?

> Avoid political incorrectness.

Nevertheless, knowledge of your audience can help

you to achieve your primary aim. So you have to do it without stereotyping them by:

- understanding the audience's knowledge level of your subject

- identifying illustrations and examples to which your audience can readily relate

- soliciting the audience's opinions and attitudes **on your subject** before you present

- ascertain the 'state-of-mind' of the audience, for instance: are you presenting to a group of highly demotivated employees?

- are there any particular words or expressions that will appeal to the audience – especially any individuals who are key to the success of your primary aim?

And, most importantly:

> Tread a careful path through the presentation to minimise (if not eliminate) the risk of offending anyone.

This need to tread carefully should also take account of the potential reactions of others who may hear of the presentation after the event.

Building a rapport

If you can establish and build rapport with an audience, they are more likely to listen to you. The more they listen, the more likely it is that they will support you in achieving your primary aim.

A fundamental in building rapport is to ensure that the audience can easily relate to the message, the messenger and the way it is delivered.

So during your preparation, it will be useful to know:

- when this audience responded well to past presentations – and when they didn't

- when the audience has given greater praise to one presenter over others

- when different methods of presenting achieved different degrees of acceptance.

If you can discover why some presentations worked better than others, learn by it.

Special needs

When researching, find out whether any member of the audience has any special needs that, in some way, may (unless you act) inhibit understanding. For example, certain people may:

- be unable to look at a projected image

- have difficulty assimilating the written word at the same speed as others

- be physically uncomfortable if expected to sit or stand in a given position for a set period of time

- have impaired hearing or eyesight

- be unable to stay comfortably in a room which has no natural daylight

- need to go to the toilet more frequently than others

None of the above suggests that any such person is either less worthy to receive your message or less able to understand it – unless, that is, you fail to respond to those needs.

In summary

- check that your primary aim matches with the expectations of your audience (and anyone who requested you to make the presentation)

- know the size of your audience

- seek the attendance of everyone needed to enable the fulfillment of your primary aim – and let them know in advance what that aim is

- the attitude of an audience can influence the style, content and structure of your presentation, so identify it early in your preparation

- audience attitudes can change within seconds of starting a presentation

- invitations should explain what individual members of the audience will gain by attending

- research the knowledge level of the audience and

their known understanding of any jargon

- avoid stereotyping your audience yet still find out everything you can about their thoughts, attitudes and opinions

- stay politically correct

- look for ways to build rapport with your audience

- research and accommodate any special needs.

4

Location, location, location!

A highly polished presentation can still fail to achieve its primary aim if the location is wrong. So what do we mean by a wrong location? Consider:

- a room that is too hot will encourage the audience to fall asleep; too cold and they could lose concentration

- a poorly lit room can strain people's eyes – too bright and it can induce headaches (and make it difficult to see projected images)

- noise from outside the room can cause as many difficulties as poor acoustics inside

- a room with spectacular views can be highly distracting, yet without windows, it can be oppressive

- a room that is too small makes people uncomfortable, if too large, it inhibits rapport building

- giving attendees tables can be great for note-taking yet detrimental to rapport (it creates a barrier)

- uncomfortable seating makes it difficult to maintain attention – too comfortable can encourage sleeping!

- wall mirrors are highly distracting for the presenters and audience alike

- columns in the middle of a room prevent eye contact.

Therefore:

> **Check the room in advance of making a presentation (if not before booking it).**

The overriding principle should be that:

> **All aspects of the location must be geared to support the presenter in achieving the primary aim.**

Choosing the location

Having completed our audience research (in the last chapter), we can now look for a location that will satisfy their numbers and be geographically convenient for them (or the majority of them).

Having chosen the general area, we should consider a specific venue next. All the warning signs in the opening section of this chapter should be considered, plus:

- do not assume that everyone has a car – can it be reached by public transport?

- can you book a specific room (rather than one of many)?

- do you need more than one room, or a reception or coffee area?

- will they provide the layout you need (see below)

- what is included in the hire – what is not? Specifically, think about equipment that you might need and materials (such as flip chart pads which sometimes are add-on charges)

- does it accommodate people with special needs?

- are there adequate health and safety provisions?

- what are the cancellation charges?

Special needs

Remember to check that all special needs of your potential audience can and will be met **without difficulty**. It is not appropriate to say to an individual person in a wheelchair, *'Don't worry – when you get there, we'll find three or four people to carry you up and down the stairs.'*

Think about everyone who may have a special need. For instance, what would an attendee do if they couldn't read the signs to the room?

Room layout

The number of attendees and the specific location may give you options as to the layout of the room. However:

> The decision on how to lay out the room should be based on what is best suited to achieve your primary aim.

Some of the factors to consider are:

- if the audience needs to make notes, tables would make sense

- if you have a large audience, a 'theatre style' layout (rows of chairs) does minimise the distance between the presenter and the back of the audience

- avoid people feeling crowded

- for a more informal approach, remove tables, although use low occasional tables for people to put down their coffee cups. A circle of chairs (perhaps laid out as in the shape of the letter 'C' – sometimes called 'u-shape') can work well

- a restaurant-style layout (that is, people sitting around a number of tables) facilitates group working, but makes eye contact with the presenter difficult. It can also make it difficult for the audience to see your visual aids.

Ensure you get written confirmation of all the details you have agreed.

Do not assume that the layout will be as you requested, so always allow time to make any necessary adjustments prior to your presentation.

Directions are always useful

A personal plea: give me a map, a set of directions from whatever compass point I travel. And, make sure it is something that can be easily read!

Remember to include directions from the local railway and bus station.

Don't just think about directions **to** the location, but also **within** it. Signage from the reception area is good – poor direction by a receptionist is dreadful.

Plan a welcome

Think about how your audience – your guests – will be met on their arrival.

As presenter, you may not have the opportunity (or the inclination) to wait around at the doorway to greet everyone. You may need someone to:

• distribute name badges and/or handouts

- guide people to their seats

- direct them to the toilets

- answer any questions they may have.

Timings at the location

Consider:

- the room's availability

- will you be able to get there before your audience in ample time to prepare?

- when thinking about when to start, consider the travelling time for the audience – what is a reasonable time for them to set out for your presentation? Will they need to rest after their journey?

- the audience may need to use public transport – what is the earliest time they can all arrive by?

- after lunch, audiences tend to tire easily. How might this impact the achievement of your primary aim?

- are you going to finish in time for your audience to reach their follow-on destinations at a reasonable time?

Arrival and start times are different – make sure you advise both. People need to know from what time they can start arriving (perhaps for a coffee) and the deadline by which they **must** arrive (which is the start of the presentation).

Refreshments

You may want to provide some refreshment on arrival, during a break or after the presentation. Arrange the refreshments at the time of booking the room. Think about:

- where the refreshments are to be served. (Do you really want lunch set up in the same room whilst you are presenting?)

- will all dietary needs be satisfied?

- how long it will take for serving, consuming and clearing food – will that fit with your timetable?

- if there are smokers, will they be accommodated (or not)?

- whether or not the availability of alcohol is advisable. If so, finish your presentation first.

First thoughts – visual aids

Chapter 7 explores visual aids in detail, but think about them now in relation to your location.

> It is the primary aim that should dictate which visual aids (if any) to use, and not the room.

First – identify the appropriate visual aids to achieve your primary aim and which can be seen by everyone in your audience.

Second – the room must suit the chosen visual aid. For example: A low ceiling can prevent the use of a projector screen, a misplaced column in the middle of the room will inhibit visibility.

Third – if your visual aids need electricity, be certain that there are enough power points located where you need them. Remember, if you are using a projector, too much light will 'fade-out' many images.

Fourth – if using sound, consider the acoustics and ensure that those at the back of the room can hear as clearly as everyone else.

Setting your 'stage'

We will now look at how your part of the room – your 'stage' – needs to be organised. Your stage might be at the same floor level as the audience – or it could literally be a stage. Whichever it is, when selecting a location you need to be sure it can work for you and your primary aim.

When setting up your stage, consider:

- will all of your audience be able to see you? If using theatre-style seating, ensure that the chairs are not directly behind one another but staggered (like you would see in a cinema) to improve visibility

- will the audience be able to hear you? Test the acoustics. Microphones could be an option (see Chapter 9)

- have you, as presenter, enough space? Too much movement is not good (you will look nervous) –

but being too static will make you look terrified! Give yourself space to move around

- will you be able to make eye contact with everyone without having to turn your back on someone else? Sometimes, it is unavoidable – but try

- have you space for your notes, visual aids and a glass of water – preferably use a low table or a desk set to one side? Lecterns are a possibility – but not one I favour (presenters tend to cling onto them like a life raft!)

Health and safety

> Every consideration must be given to health and safety issues when preparing for and making a presentation.

The potential list of issues here is vast and prioritising what I perceive to be the greatest risks is dangerous. So I won't.

I will, however, say two things:

- it is vital that the room can be evacuated easily without obstruction (and the audience is told how to do so)

- the setting up of the room introduces all sorts of hazards into that room – not least the dangers of tripping over or bumping into equipment, wires etc. Think about it.

Ensure that all hazards are identified, managed and, where necessary, advised to the audience.

In summary

- check out the location in advance – there are too many variables which can inhibit success

- choosing a location should be dependent upon your needs as presenter in achieving your primary aim

- a location needs to be accessible to all of the audience, including those with special needs

- lay the room out to provide you with a 'stage' area and the audience with the space and furnishings to be comfortable – but not too comfortable!

- make sure that the details of any location are agreed in writing

- give the audience clear directions on how to get to your location

- plan how your audience will be greeted upon arrival

- think carefully about appropriate arrival, start and finish times for the audience and yourself

- include any refreshment arrangements at the time of booking

- preferably, choose the visual aids you will need before determining a location

- always bear in mind the health and safety needs of the audience and the presenter.

5

The audience doesn't always listen

Even a positive audience doesn't hear everything the presenter says. Why? Well perhaps for the best of reasons – you have spoken such thought-provoking words that they are doing exactly what you wanted – thinking. But if they are thinking – or making notes – they can't listen as effectively.

People also stop listening because they are tired, daydreaming, thinking about something else or bored. To minimise the consequences of people not listening effectively (which includes misunderstandings or a total lack of understanding) we need to create an effective structure.

> A structure helps the audience to understand.

Structure and 'signposts'

A structure gives the audience opportunities to 're-join' the presentation if they lose their way – these can be called 'signposts'.

Imagine the presentation as an unfamiliar car journey. Every now and again, you check where you are and, using the signposts, move on to the next part of the journey. So it should be with a presentation. For example:

'Okay, we have dealt with the various government grants available to you, now we will move on to show how you can apply for them ...'

The presenter has summarised (briefly) where they have got up to and where they are going next. They have signposted the way. Anyone who lost track up to that point, can now rejoin for the rest of it.

All structures need signposts.

Basic rules of structure

Start by identifying the information that you **must** communicate to achieve your primary aim (see Chapter 2). Ideally, there would be no more than five or six key points. These points are your paragraph headings, under which you can write the detail.

To illustrate, let's say that I am presenting on how to prepare for a presentation. My key points (or headings) will be: the aim, content, audience, location, structure and visual aids.

Taking the first heading (the aim), we might say:

'First we will look at creating the primary aim for your presentation. Write down what it is you want to achieve and then identify as many success criteria as possible. There are some key questions that will help you in identifying that aim ...'

And as we reach the end of the paragraph, we will close with a signpost:

'... so that is how to define the primary aim. We will now build on this by moving onto the second key point – that of researching the content of the presentation.'

Try to discuss each key point for approximately the same length of time. If you do, it says that each point is of the same importance and spaces your signposts evenly. Further, if you spend a disproportionate half an hour on the first of six points, the audience will calculate that it will take you three hours to finish. They will immediately feel tired! If a key point is much longer than the others, sub-divide it into two or more.

Arguably it is better to make the last point slightly shorter in length. The audience knows you are nearly finished and may start looking forward to stretching their legs, going to the toilet or whatever.

Finally, ensure the key points are in a logical sequence.

> The basic structural rule is therefore:Present key points of roughly equal duration in a logical sequence.

The beginning

> All presentations must have a *beginning*, *middle* and *end* irrespective of your chosen structure.

So what **must** you include in the beginning?

- a welcome, a greeting

- an introduction of yourself. This is not your life-history! Keep it succinct and relevant to your primary aim – for example:
  'Good afternoon, everyone. My name is Brian Lomas and I am here, as the author of the easy step by step guide on making confident presentations, to ...'

- outline your **primary aim**: what are you there to achieve? (You may not reveal all of your aim – you wouldn't, for instance, say that one of your success criteria is to get wild applause at the end of your presentation!) To continue with our example:
  '... give you as many tips and hints as I can on preparing for a presentation to enable you to feel more confident in the future ...'

- next, we need to manage their expectations on how long you are going to talk. Always give the maximum time – to finish early is acceptable, to overrun, unforgivable:
  '... over the next 20 minutes ...'

- now, we need something that will encourage the audience to start listening. This 'wake-up call' states what they will gain from giving your presentation their full attention. It could be a **positive** wake-up or a **negative** one:
  *'... and thereby ensure that you get what you want out of your presentations ...' **(positive)**

or:

'... and thus avoid those tears and tantrums you may well experience just before starting a presentation ...' **(negative)**

- next, outline how you will be approaching the subject (your structure and your key points that you **must** communicate):

  '... I'll describe these tools under six headings – namely the aim, content, audience, location, structure and visual aids.'

The beginning might also include:

- domestic arrangements: your audience must be told the evacuation procedures; they should be told where the toilets are; break times; refreshment arrangements; smoking rules, and how messages for the audience will be dealt with

- a request for your audience to turn off their mobile phones whenever possible

- let the audience know when you would like to take questions. If you don't do this, be prepared for questions at the most awkward of times! (See Chapter 8 for more on questions)

- the information sources upon which your presentation is based

- Background to the presentation: although not essential, it may be useful for the audience to know why the presentation is being made. If this cannot be done briefly, consider making it the first point in the middle part of the structure

  'Can everyone hear and see me?' The only reason

that this is not listed as essential is that it would look a little odd if you only had three people in your audience!

- To dispel presenter nerves, it **can** be useful to encourage some involvement by the audience at an early stage. Think about this carefully – if the involvement backfires (they could give you different responses to those you anticipate – or no answers at all), it is likely to increase your nervousness!

> Don't skimp on the beginning – it gives people time to adjust to your voice and settle into your presentation.

The middle

There are many ways to structure the middle of a presentation but remember that the structure is based on key points being presented in a logical sequence with signposts along the way. Plus:

> All structures should enable the audience to easily understand the presentation.

Five themes you could use to structure the middle part of your presentation are:

- progressive

- narrative

- analytical

- persuasive

- picture-painting.

We will now look at each of these in more detail.

Progressive theme

The simplest, this sequences the key points, typically starting at the earliest point chronologically.

You could say: *'This is where we are, I'm now going to describe from the beginning how we got here.'*

Some other examples of progressive themes would be:

- describing expenditure from zero to the current situation

- explaining quality initiatives which have enhanced each previous improvement

- an escalation of events to reach a climax.

Narrative theme

Tell a story. Remember, however, it is the message in the story that you want the audience to recall, not the story itself.

Rarely will a real-life story suit the exact needs of a primary aim (unless the aim is to tell the story itself), so be prepared to elaborate, simplify or change the sequence of events to achieve your primary aim.

Do not tell an incomplete story (nor run out of time) – you can't leave the audience wondering what happened next. And do beware of losing track of your primary aim – you could get 'carried away' in your storytelling.

Analytical theme
To present an analysis of a subject, you can either:

* look at the same subject from a number of different perspectives

or

* map the analysis process step by step until the end result is achieved.

For example, in analysing poor sales performance, we could look at it from the customer's perspective, new and established product ranges, the sales trends in relation to complaints, a change in margins, etc. This would open up the subject for discussion.

Alternatively, we could analyse poor sales performance by narrowing down the area in decline. So, we may discover that it is the new product range that is suffering. Further investigation into these new products show that it is the sales of Product X that are poor. When we analyse that, we might find that the main purchaser of Product X has financial problems.

Choosing the right type of analytical structure will be dependent upon your primary aim.

Include a (brief) description of the analytical tool or tools you are using at each stage.

Persuasive theme

Adopt this theme to influence or sell (products, services or ideas). It is useful in securing agreement as to why a set of recommendations (perhaps a decision) should be supported.

This theme takes the audience through a series of statements to which they will be in full agreement. It will deal with any likely problems upfront and end in a position where the audience has been led to only one conclusion – which just so happens to be that reflected in your primary aim. For good measure, we will also try to motivate the audience into agreement.

For example (in abbreviated form):

'I believe that any car which you may buy for your company fleet needs to be reliable...' **(something the would-be purchaser identified earlier and therefore is agreeable)**

'... and very cost-efficient...' **(again, gleaned from earlier conversations and now building on areas of agreement)**

'... that way you can be sure of getting your people to their meetings with customers without mechanical problems and without it costing too much ...' **(using what the purchaser was talking about earlier to motivate them to act)**

'... You may wish to look at these independent industry statistics which state that the resale value holds better than any of our major competitors ...' **(in response to a potential problem the purchaser voiced earlier)**

'Finally, our cars have received the best feedback from drivers in a recent survey – so there is no doubt your colleagues will see your decision to buy these cars as a

very, very good one.' **(Appealing to this purchaser's individual motivation to be liked by their colleagues)**

To close (following any questions), **ask for their agreement and wait for their answer**.

The 'trick' here is having a series of statements with which the audience agree – it is then very difficult for them to suddenly say 'no' at the end. The close of the presentation is saying that there really is no alternative – it just **has** to be the one you are recommending.

Picture-painting theme

This structure is most apt when you need to bring together information to achieve your primary aim for which there is no apparent sequence.

For example:

Let's assume that your primary aim requires that you need to describe the layout and decoration of a room. We could describe the floor, then the ceiling **and its relationship with the floor**, next the furniture by the window **and its relationship to the ceiling and floor**. And so on.

When you have finished, your audience should be able to visualise the whole 'picture' you have described.

The ending

First, we must indicate that we have arrived at the end of the middle and are about to start the beginning of the end! You could use one of a number of phrases to do this.

For example:

- 'In summary then ...'

- 'So that concludes the key points of ...'

- 'Before I move towards closing the presentation ...'

Follow this with a summary of the key points you have presented (the must-do headings) to ensure the audience does not forget them.

What else might we include in the end?

- sources of further information on the subject (but do not give new information)

- an opportunity for questions (see Chapter 8)

- a re-statement of your aim and that it has been achieved (do not doubt it – you must convey the belief that you have succeeded!)

- an emphasis on what you want the audience to do as a result of the presentation

- a thank you to the audience for listening

And most importantly:

> **Close on a highly positive statement.**

Whet the appetite or give them a feast?

So should a presentation leave the audience wanting more? Or should you give them everything that they might dream of from this presentation?

Well, the answer is a bit of both. Give the audience everything they are looking for – and a bit extra. Yet leave them wanting more, if only time permitted.

In summary

- remember that the audience will not be listening to every word

- **signposts** during a presentation help an audience to keep track of where you are up to as well as enabling any that have 'turned-off' to re-join the presentation

- presentations should have a structure to facilitate understanding

- all structures should state what <u>must</u> be communicated in the beginning and the middle and the end

- the middle of the presentation should have a logical sequence of key points of roughly equal duration – but not too many to cause information overload

- five themes for the middle of a presentation are: progressive, narrative, analytical, persuasive and picture-painting

- close on a highly positive statement – having exceeded their expectations, but wanting yet more.

6

To script or not to script?

It can be said that a script stilts the flow of the presenter and reduces eye contact (and therefore rapport). This, however, distorts the purpose of a script.

For example, a cinema film will have a script to which the actors and actresses adhere. They don't use the script in sight of the audience, but they would have been lost without it at the start of rehearsals. So it is with presentations.

> Only if a script exists can an effective presentation be created, the flow developed and it's duration estimated.

That, however, does not mean that we should **never** use that script in front of an audience. There will be occasions when reading from a script is advisable (for instance, when delivering a message which is 'word-sensitive', such as a statement to the press or the Stock Exchange).

There are, however, times when a script is inappropriate:

- the greater the audience participation, the less feasible a script will be (since you, as presenter, can't anticipate specific responses from the audience)

- if your speech is 'from the heart'. For example: A declaration of love to your sweetheart would seem to lose its appeal if you needed a script!

- if you have been given five minutes' notice of a presentation, there will be no time to write a script – but prompts are still possible.

Do not be fooled by people who appear never to use a script or prompts. They will have thought very carefully about what they were going to say. And they may have a superb memory.

The benefits of scripting are that it ensures:

- nothing is missed

- a flow is established

- irrelevant information is discarded

- rehearsals are feasible (you can't rehearse something that is constantly changing)

- a reasonable estimate of the presentation's duration can be made.

The script

Keep your primary aim visible throughout the script-writing process so that you don't write anything that is irrelevant. Write everything that you are going to say – starting with 'Good afternoon, thank you for coming ...'

> **When developing a script, write as you would speak.**

If you are **given** a script, ask if you can translate it into your own words – and if so, do it. If you have to deliver someone else's script word-for-word, be certain that you understand it. Rehearse it thoroughly – ideally with the scriptwriter who can ensure that it conveys the meaning they want.

Rehearse with the script and gradually reduce it to a series of 'prompts'.

Prompts to be wary of

- a 'tele-prompter'. These are not prompts at all but a script on a television screen – rather like a karaoke machine. Having said all that, with much practice, they can be used to great effect

- large cards held up in front of you. These will only work for the very shortest of speeches!

- an 'off-stage' prompter (as in a theatre). Again, you would need to stick rigidly to the script and can run the danger of being distracted by it. Plus, can they whisper loud enough for you to hear – but not the audience?

Recommended prompts

Value your prompts. If you throw them aside when you have finished talking, you are 'inviting' the audience to do the same with their notes.

Three types of prompts are recommended. You can use more than one for a single presentation.

• **Bulleted text**
Shorten the script into bullet points. You should include key words and phrases, statistics, quotations – especially those you might forget.

This will help you to remember what to say and, because you are not reading a script, you can still maintain eye contact and build rapport with the audience. The amount of information you 'bullet' will depend upon how comfortable you feel after your rehearsals.

Bulleted prompts should always include the information you must communicate to achieve your primary aim.

• **Cribs**
These are a bit like the slips of paper students try to sneak in to exams! Not that you ever considered such a thing – but you may have heard of it happening.

First, to be clear, I am **not** suggesting that you write

on your shirt-sleeves or fill your stage area with tatty pieces of paper! I *am* suggesting, however, that you should:

- regard all visual aids as prompts: if projecting text onto a screen, that text may well be all the prompting you need

- if using a flip chart, pre-write prompts on each page in pencil (faintly) so you can read it and your audience can't (check!)

- if using overhead projector acetates, buy frames for these slides and write further prompts (to the text) on these frames.

- **Diagrams**

Frequently a one-page prompt:

- **spider diagrams**: in the centre of the page, write the subject of the presentation and then draw lines outwards to each of the key points. Link sub-points, as necessary, with further lines.

Alternatively:

- A **flow diagram**: summarise the presentation as a series of text statements linked with arrows.

There will always be the possibility that, when standing in front of your audience, your cribs and prompts fail to give you enough information. Don't panic! Instead:

Always have two versions of what you intend to say – the one you are going to use and a more detailed version.

Ensure both are at hand during your presentation.

Avoid losing your way

To help you to avoid losing your place (especially after looking away from your prompts):

- space out the text

- ensure text is of a size that you can read easily. Do you need to use reading glasses? (It will be distracting if you keep taking them off to 'see' the audience and putting them on to read your prompts)

- upper and lowercase text is easier to read than uppercase alone

- highlight key words (choose a colour that can be seen clearly)

- use a (wide) margin for timings and perhaps 'stage-directions'. For example: *'Display the pre-prepared flip chart'*

- consider using columns: one for the information you **must** communicate; in the next, related items you **should** communicate; in the third what you **could** say

- if you are using more than one piece of paper (or card) for your prompts:

  number each page

  use a new page for each key point (to stop pausing inappropriately midway through a point)

  write on one side only (you could lose track of whether or not to turn over)

  attach the pages with loose string or a 'treasury tag' (if they fall, they won't get mixed up).

> If you forget to say something, you are probably the only one that knows.
>
> Move on.
>
> If it is important, you will find a way to talk about it – perhaps when taking questions.

Handouts

Handouts should not be copies of your script – with the possible exception of press releases and other carefully worded statements.

Handouts are:

- key facts included in your presentation

And/or

- information that is supplemental to your presentation

Handouts may not always be necessary.

> Ask yourself: *'Will the audience remember what I am saying without handouts?'*

You could ask the audience to make their own notes, but you have no control over what they might or might not write down, nor whether they write it down accurately. If they do make notes (give them pen and paper), you might have to speak more slowly to give people time to write or copy (from the visual aids).

Let's consider some guidelines on when handouts would be a good idea:

- to allow people to quote from them in the future (this could also be a reason **not** to issue handouts)

- to allow non-attendees to read what they missed

- to convey detail

- when there is insufficient time for you to present everything you want to.

And if you decide on handouts:

- your presentation and the handouts must be consistent

- if reproducing the visual aids (without supplementary information), check they make sense as a stand-alone document

- check the quality by thorough proofreading.

Distribution of handouts
Your options are:

- **in advance of the presentation**: this gives people time to read and think about the subject and therefore encourages questions and discussion. It will make no difference, however, if they haven't read it!

  Your presentation should give something over and above that written in the handouts – or there would be no reason for anyone to attend.

- **at the start of the presentation**: this helps people who want notes for later reflection. They will only need to make supplemental notes and can therefore listen more attentively. However, people tend to read (or skim-read) ahead of the presenter, which can be very distracting

- **during the presentation**: not recommended unless the handouts directly relate to a stage in your presentation where you want the audience to break from listening (for instance, to start a discussion). It will disrupt your flow as presenter and be difficult for the audience to settle down again

- **after the presentation**: tell the audience in your introduction that you are going to distribute handouts (and therefore whether or not they would be advised to take notes).

In determining when to distribute handouts, ask:
'When will best serve my primary aim?'

In summary

- scripts should be written in full – but rarely used during the presentation itself

- seek permission to use your own words if given a script by someone else

- be wary of tele-prompters, large prompt cards and side-stage theatre-style prompters

- value your prompts – be they bulleted text, crib notes or diagrams

- write prompts in a way to minimise the chance of losing your way

- if you forget to say something, move on. You are probably the only person who knows that it has been missed and if it is that important, you will find a way to say it later

- use handouts if they support your primary aim and think about when will be the best time to distribute them.

7

Choose your visuals

People can get bored with visuals – even the humming noise of a projector can irritate after a while.

So should you use visual aids at all – and, if so, which ones? Here are some guidelines:

- they should never detract from your presentation

- the more you use, the more it confuses your audience and fragments your presentation

- the larger the audience, the more restricted will be your choice (they have to be able to see!)

- they should suit your audience's expectations

- they should work in your location (in Chapter 4, I advocated that the location should be chosen **after** you have chosen your visuals, but this is not always possible).

The overriding principle here is:

> You should only use visual aids that will help you achieve your primary aim.

Controlling visual aids

You must stay in control. Felt tip pens dry up, projector bulbs burn out, computers crash. Be prepared – **anything** could happen!

Hide visuals from view when not relevant to a specific point in your presentation. This doesn't mean that you should remove equipment – rather that, when appropriate, the audience should have nothing else to look at but you. So change a flip chart pad to a blank page and don't leave a screen image on after you have finished with it.

Visual aids – the equipment

The basic types are:

- **overhead projector**: electrically powered, this uses light and mirrors to project an image from the horizontal onto a vertical (or near vertical) screen. These images are usually pre-printed on A4 acetate slides. Suitable for small and medium size audiences

- **computer-linked projector**: this has become **the** professional visual aid. Images can be projected from behind or in front of the screen. Front pro-jectors can be ceiling-mounted (allowing unob-structed vision for the audience) or from a table or stand. Suitable for any size of audience although it might appear 'over-the-top' for small groups

- **flip chart easels** with A1 writing pads. Although not always the most stable piece of equipment, they are highly flexible and (usually) benefit from a sloping writing surface to ease use. Ideal for small groups and perhaps medium ones – its readability being dependent on the size and neatness of your writing. If pre-preparing flip charts, be aware that different easels have different methods of suspend-ing the paper – are they compatible?

- **Wipe-boards and blackboards**: these are usually fitted vertically to a wall and are not as easy to use as a sloping surface. Since the requisite writing tools are 'wipe-clean', you could accidentally wipe/smudge it as you write. Always use the right felt tip pens – permanent ink is difficult to remove without a special cleaner. Suitable for small to medium audiences, again dependent upon your writing size and neatness

- **video players** (and a television!): always cue the tape in advance. Check the volume – some televi-sions do not operate well if the volume is turned too high. If presenting to large groups, bring in the professional stage crews!

There are, in addition, new technologies for visual aids being developed all the time – the key rule is that whatever you decide to use, keep practicing until you can deal with the unexpected!

Setting up your equipment

> **Always set equipment up in advance.**

Some tips:

- know how the equipment works. Where are the on/off buttons? How do you stop the video-player tape? How do you change bulbs?

- if you need electricity – make sure you have enough **working** power points close enough to your stage

- if using a projector linked to a computer, be certain that the combination works together as one set piece. (I once hired a lap top computer complete with loaded software and a projector – asking the supplier to ensure it worked. It didn't – but I had allowed time to rectify it)

- lower lighting levels make projected images easier to read. Some projector bulbs are weaker than others (and therefore do not project images as clearly)

- consider angling projector screens across a corner of your stage to improve visibility. If the top of your image is wider than the lower when projected, tilt the top of the screen forward. (Screens frequently have an angle bar to enable you to do this)

- sit in different parts of the room to check that your images can be seen clearly

- flip chart easels frequently have variable heights – is it the right height for you and your audience? And have you enough paper?

- if you doubt your ability to quickly rectify any equipment problems, consider having on-site back-up available.

And most importantly:

> **Have you set up the equipment to protect your health and safety and that of your audience?**

Using the equipment

- never 'hold-on' to equipment (or a lectern) like a security blanket!

- turning off an overhead projector when changing acetates can look tidier. However, if you **must** use a large amount of acetates, turning the machine on and off will irritate. In such a case, use computer-generated images rather than the overhead projector

- computer-linked projectors can take a while to warm up – be ready before your audience arrives. They may be timed to go to 'stand-by' after a period of inactivity – be ready for it!

Pre-developed visuals

Pre-developed visuals with text and/or graphics could be:

- on A4 acetate slides (for use with an overhead projector)

- projected from a computer: these images can include videos and potentially 'live' websites – although I would avoid the latter since, apart from being more technical, there are more things that can go wrong. The easy alternative here is to have the website loaded onto CD – and use that to project onto the screen (be wary of infringing copyright)

- stand-alone video clips, films and 35mm slides

- pre-written flip chart pages.

Pre-prepared visuals have the advantage of:

- assisting you to maintain a flow and structure throughout your presentation

- prompting you, the presenter, with what to talk about next

- allowing more time for eye contact with your audience

- being tidier or neater than something written during the presentation.

However, the disadvantages to pre-prepared visuals are:

- you may find it difficult to react to any input from the audience

- it can be difficult to eliminate content you decide (for whatever reason) not to include

- videos, if prolonged, can send an audience to sleep – and 10 minutes can be too long in some cases!

- should your visuals not be custom-made for your presentation, their relevance to the audience might be lost. (I once saw a financial marketing presentation include a photo of an iguana. Then, as now, its purpose was lost on me!).

> Triple-check your spelling on pre-prepared visuals!

Free-flowing visuals

If you prefer to develop the visuals as the presentation evolves, the alternatives are:

- writing on blank acetates (with an overhead projector)

- using flip charts, wipe-boards or blackboards

- I have yet to see effective use via computers, but dependent upon your 'typing-in-public' skills, I'm sure that day will come.

The advantages here are:

- you can write down input from your audience

- it increases the likelihood of participation by an audience, and, in turn, improves their attention span.

But they also have disadvantages:

- you will lose eye-contact when writing

- they can be untidy

- however good a speller you are, spelling mistakes are a major hazard

- if using acetates, they can be difficult to read if the ink isn't dark enough or the projector bulb not bright enough.

> Irrespective of whether or not your visuals are developed in advance of a presentation, you must still prepare them thoroughly.

Format of visuals

On page 79 are some guidelines for projected images.

This visual, however, is somewhat lacking in appeal – it can be improved by:

- adding graphics or charts

- using colour – dark backgrounds with light coloured letters can ease reading and 'projectability'

Layout of Visuals

- adopt a landscape rather than portrait format – it fits on the screen better

- Always have a heading

- Bullet points work better than prose

- Keep the font size large – as a guide, have a maximum of 7 or 8 lines of text

We could also add the presentation's title, date and any copyright messages to the footer of each slide – although this will restrict future usage. Numbering slides can help the presenter keep track, but the audience might notice if you miss one out!

Poor images would include projecting poor-quality photocopies or simply putting too much on the screen at one time.

For flip charts, the layout principles are broadly the same as with projected images, except:

- they will be portrait rather than landscape

- faint pencil lines (if using blank paper) can help you write in a straight line

- 'normal' handwriting can be difficult to read – avoid 'joined-up' lettering

- use strong blue or green inks for the main text and red ink for 'bullets' and headings.

Most importantly:

> **Do not overdo the styling.**
>
> **It must not detract from the message.**

Keeping the audience on the point

To prevent an audience reading the whole visual before you are ready:

- conceal the lower part of an acetate slide with a piece of paper over the text you are not ready for. Weight this paper down (to prevent it blowing away) by taping a ruler to it

- You can 'build' a projected computer image by pre-programming the presentation. You project the first part of the text and, upon pressing a button, the next point will be projected. Another button press, another point – and so on. To know when you have reached the last point, end the text on this last line with a full-stop

- You can automatically time computer presentations, so text will appear at set times. You will need to rehearse thoroughly to keep pace with the visual

- Pointing at the screen is to be avoided. The presenter should read from either the acetate or the computer to avoid turning your back on the audience.

3D visuals

Another type of visual is the 3D variety. Let's look at demonstrations first:

You could be demonstrating something to the audience from your stage. No problem here – providing:

- the audience is small enough so they can all see (although this can be overcome with a camera projecting your image on a screen)

- your demonstration works!

Alternatively, you could distribute demonstration models to the audience. Very dangerous! You can easily lose control, whilst the audience 'plays' with the demonstrations.

The other type of 3D visual is what we might call 'stage-props'. These could include:

- To convey an image wearing some kind of clothing or uniform. I've seen a presenter successfully promoting airline sales wearing a flying jacket. (Beware of patronising or stereotyping people offensively however)

- To portray a role – impersonators are masters of this art – they put on a pair of glasses and become another person. (I would suggest, however, that to mimic a 'real' person should not be done unless you have the skill to carry it off)

- To enliven a topic. Perhaps a model car when talking about cars (assuming it isn't appropriate to use another 3D visual – the car itself).

A box of tricks

Assume that the worst can happen. You are in the middle of your presentation and someone needs writing paper, another wants a pen, your felt tip pens dry up and you have just tripped on a cable that is dangerously stretching across from a power point.

Forethought can help you overcome many of these potential risks by having 'a box of tricks'. The content of my box includes: writing paper, pens, pencils, pencil sharpener, erasers, permanent ink marker pens, wipe board pens and cleaning pads, ruler, masking tape, scissors, stapler and staples, a calculator, etc.

And it doesn't end there: I also carry cough sweets, sticking plasters, headache pills, tissues – all just in case. I will not run the risk of losing my voice, nor suffering from a headache minutes before I start without being prepared!

And if there are no visuals...

Well there will always be at least one – you, the presenter. As sole visual aid, the eyes of the audience will be on you all the time and that can add to the pressure you feel. Presenting without other visual aids, however, can make for the most powerful of presentations. We will look at presenting yourself in later chapters.

In summary

- only choose visual aids (if at all) that support your primary aim

- be prepared – anything can go wrong. If you can't fix the most probable risks, have someone available who can

- check that the audience will be able to see and hear your visual aids clearly

- set up visual aids before your audience arrives

- prepare and rehearse with visual aids thoroughly – and quality check them before use

- you are your most important visual aid.

8

Asking your audience to participate

The more your audience participates, the more attentive they will be. (Think of how alert you would be if you had to sit quietly and listen to someone talk for hour upon hour!)

So participation is good. Or at least it is for most presentations. You may choose not to go that route if, for instance:

- you have insufficient time or the presentation is relatively short

- your message is better if delivered and then followed through at another time with participation when the audience has had time to think.

Types of participation

The most obvious is to take questions. You could also:

- ask the audience to do something relatively

straightforward – perhaps shake hands with the person sitting behind them

- divide the audience into smaller groups to consider a question (posed by you) for later feedback

- distribute handouts for them to read through, or perhaps write personal input

- let them 'play' with demonstration models (see Chapter 7)

Irrespective of your wishes, the audience might choose for themselves to participate by:

- asking questions when you have not invited them to do so

- cheer, laugh, applaud

- heckle.

Taking questions

Questions are the best way to get audience participation. Refusing questions is not advised – the audience will either believe that you have something to hide or that you are running scared.

Say in your introduction when you want questions:

- **During your presentation**: this is a good way for the audience to check their on-going understanding, but runs the risk of a time overrun or asking about a point you have planned to discuss later

- **at a time near the end** (when signalled by you). Here, the presenter can manage time effectively, but runs the risk that the audience may have stopped listening after a point they failed to understand (because they weren't given the opportunity to ask you about it).

When you ask for questions, it may take a few seconds for the audience to switch from listening-mode to that of participation. Give them a little time to adjust.

If you don't get any questions when you have asked for them, (silently count to six to give them some time), try starting them off with:

'A question I was asked just before I started was ...'

or

'The most frequently asked question I get on this subject is ...'

This 'trick' can also be used to introduce a key piece of information that you might have forgotten about during the presentation. Ask yourself a question to which your answer would be the information you need to convey.

Answering questions – basic rules

- listen to the whole question before answering

- welcome the question (perhaps *'Thank you'* or *'That's a good question ...'*)

- check you understand the question: if you are unsure, ask

- repeat (or paraphrase) the question so the audience can all hear it and to check you have understood. This also gives you time to think of the answer!

- pause to give the impression that it is worthy of consideration

- answer it succinctly, relate it to your presentation yet give some new/additional information to encourage further questions. Do not make them feel that they should have listened more closely to you.

Answering questions – hints and tips

- if you don't understand the relevance to your presentation, ask them to explain it

- it can be good practice to check with the questioner whether or not you have answered their question. Be prepared, however, for them to say you haven't!

- do not start a conversation with a questioner

- if you don't know, say so! Promise to find out the answer and get back to them within a timeframe to which you must seek their active agreement – perhaps:

  'The short answer is that I don't know. If you could let me have your contact details at the end of the presentation, I will find out the answer and I will get back to you by the end of next week. Would that be okay?'

  Have a notepad (or a volunteer) ready to make appropriate notes – this also emphasises to the audience your intention to respond

- never let their attitude encroach on yours: you must be seen (and heard) to welcome each question – so if a questioner is aggressive, stay calm

- if the question is difficult to answer or you can't immediately think of an answer, try taking a sip from a glass of water (one of the presenter's most useful props). It buys you a few valuable seconds to think. One ploy you can use is to ask the audience what their views are and then take parts of their answers to express your 'own' opinion

- answer 'hypothetical' questions with care – they may not be hypothetical at all

- avoid single word answers, however if the questioner is asking for a yes/no answer, it can be very powerful if you say 'yes' or 'no' and then follow it up with your reasoning

- if one member of the audience persists in asking questions, you need to involve other members. Ask: *'Has anyone else got a question they would like to ask?'*

> Think about likely (especially awkward) questions and appropriate answers during your preparation.

In reality, it is unlikely that you will think of all the questions you might be asked. If you adopted the method in Chapter 2 of sorting information into what **must**, **should** and **could** be communicated, the answers to most questions will be found within the 'could' communicate category.

Closing question time

> Remember to allocate time for questions –
> and stick to that time.

Should you take questions towards the end of your presentation, always have a positive closing statement worked out to finish with. This ensures that no matter how tough the questions have been, your presentation will end positively.

> Always have the last word after questions to
> end on a high.

Humour

Humour can, through laughter, involve the audience. It can also backfire – before including humour in your presentation, ask:

- can I create laughter without fear of offending anyone in the audience?

- is humour conducive to the style of my presentation, its primary aim and the expectations of my audience?

- can I really get away with telling a joke that I heard in the bar after a few drinks?

And most importantly:

> **Can I, as presenter, recover if the audience does *not* laugh at my humour?**

Having said this, the presenter's ability to use humour and/or laugh at oneself can be invaluable. For instance:

I remember watching Harold Wilson, the then Prime Minister making a speech. He started by saying that just before he came on stage, he noticed a button was missing off his suit jacket. Had he not mentioned it, the audience might notice and doubt his attention to detail or his suitability to represent the UK. So – what did he do? He brought everyone's attention to it and cracked a joke at his own expense. No, I don't remember the joke (sorry), but the point is that he portrayed himself as a fallible human being who could laugh at himself – an attribute that many tend to admire in a politician.

Political correctness

The previous story and appropriateness of humour leads nicely into mentioning political correctness. For some, the world has gone too far in being politically correct – but for others it has not gone far enough.

For example, I listened to a lady presenter discuss a hypothetical situation. A manager was discussing the need for improved performance with a staff member. Okay so far. Until, that is, the hypothetical manager became a 'he' and the member of staff a 'she'.

Since when are all managers male? Maybe the men in the audience felt more secure, maybe the ladies in the audience comfortable with the stereotyping. Who knows? The point is that it may have offended someone and thus the presenter may well have lost the support of some in the audience before even reaching the end of the presentation. So, albeit that pedantic adherence to correctness can irritate (for instance, saying 'he or she' all the time):

> A presenter should always stay politically correct.

Handling hecklers

Some politicians love being heckled – it brings out their best. Many others will hate me for saying this!

I have seen very different responses to hecklers. To totally ignore them and continue with the presentation becomes a battle of wills (who can speak loudest?) and yet stopping the presentation until they finish (if they do finish, that is) is giving them exactly what they want – your audience's attention.

So you need to do something in response to hecklers. Above all, stay calm. The most successful tactic I have seen (short of having the heckler removed!) is one where the presenter catches the gist of the heckled message and then responds along the lines of:

'Someone in the audience wants to know what I think about (for instance) capital punishment. Well I'll tell you if you'll listen ...'

A follow-up tactic to persistent heckling can be:

'You will have your turn to speak as much as you want later – after I have finished. I'm sure the audience will stay on to listen to any valid point that you feel needs to be made ...'

Avoid a conversation with the heckler. Any response you give to the issue they are raising should be addressed to the audience and not involve the heckler.

I have seen presenters verbally attack hecklers for poor manners or their lack of magnetism in securing an audience of their own, so they set out to steal someone else's. But I haven't seen this work successfully without a follow-up eviction from the room.

Responding with a smile can work, however:

'I know I am hitting the mark with my comments when someone decides to heckle me ...'

In summary

- audience participation is good providing it serves your primary aim

- tell the audience in the introduction when you would like questions and prepare answers to those you can think of – especially the awkward ones!

- listen carefully to the question and check that you understand

- be succinct and honest in your replies

- always have the last word after questions to end on a high

- humour can be very effective but it can also be dangerous: think about whether or not you will readily recover from a failed attempt at humour, and stay politically correct

- if heckling is a possibility, devise in advance a strategy to cope with it.

9
You are a visual aid

Make an entrance

An audience can be quite brutal in taking a dislike to a presenter before they have even said a word – and that will inhibit your success. So how you enter the room and act before you start is crucial.

> **First impressions count.**
>
> **Make them work in your favour.**

So what impression must you give? Well, you must show that:

- **you are well prepared**: all of your notes, equipment and the 'stage' should be organised before your audience enter the room. If you are following a previous presenter and have to reset the stage in front of the audience, do it quickly and calmly before you start speaking

- **you should exude confidence and calmness** (however you might feel inside)

- when you are ready to start, **'take' the stage**. Walk to the centre of the stage, stop, face the audience and await their attention. Try to avoid shouting over any chatter to gain attention – your stage 'presence' should be enough to do this. Walking to centre-stage in a curve rather than a straight line has the advantage of saying 'I have arrived' (and will avoid signalling that you would rather keep walking in a straight line right out of the room!)

Your appearance

There are a few obvious things to start with here:

- you should be well-groomed

- are your clothes comfortable? Do not wear brand new clothes at a presentation – you don't know whether or not the buttons and zips are reliable! And new shoes sometimes squeak – so wear what you know

- do not distract the audience with your appearance. For instance: jewellery can catch the light or move about too much (such as a loose, sparkling bracelet) and avoid clothes with printed wording or 'cartoons' (your audience will be distracted trying to read it)

- ensure your appearance is 'fit for the purpose'. You may need to move about the stage, bend down, twist around – will your clothes and hairstyle stay in place?

Having said this, how smart should you be?

> **Wear clothes a little smarter than the audience to show respect.**

If you are too smart (or too scruffy), you could make some of the audience uncomfortable. Think in advance about how the audience are likely to dress.

Being heard

You need to project your voice so that you can be heard clearly by anyone with poor hearing or at the back of the room. (Chapter 3 discussed the need for you to identify anyone with special hearing needs and re-spond accordingly).

Talk to an imaginary person *behind* those furthest away from you and if you speak loud enough for that imaginary person to hear, so could most others.

To project your voice:

- **keep your chin up** (looking down at notes will suppress the power of your voice)

- **look at the audience** not, for instance, your vi-sual aids. If you must turn away from the audi-ence, stop talking

- **talk more slowly than normal**, especially at the beginning. This allows the audience to 'tune-in' to your voice, rather like tuning in a radio. They need to adjust their listening – and you need to give them the chance to do so

- **do not shout**: the 'voice' you should use is akin to coaxing a child or a dog to come to you from some distance – without fear of being chastised

- **don't worry about your accent** unless it is very strong and unusual for your audience (in which case consider moderating it)

- **emphasise key words and phrases** with your voice. In Chapter 2, we discussed what you ***must*** communicate to achieve your primary aim. To emphasise these points say them a little louder and slower than usual. For the points that you ***should*** communicate, use your normal presenting voice. For that which you ***could*** communicate, a slightly softer, quicker voice is appropriate. All of this will put variety in your voice and makes it easier to listen to

- **long sentences** can mean you will run out of breath and your voice will lose its strength, so use short sentences

- if you **raise the pitch** of your voice at the end of sentences, it will help you to maintain your voice projection.

Microphones

Should you be unable to project your voice to the back of the room, a microphone will be needed:

- practice using it before the audience arrives

- make sure you know how to use the on/off button

- use your normal volume of voice (but, as already stated, without losing the pitch or pace variance)

- if a static microphone, avoid varying the distance between you and it

- if being fitted with a radio microphone, be aware that you will need to be 'wired-up' and carry a transmitter. Wear appropriate clothes.

Silence is power

If you pause while speaking, it *says 'I have just made an important point, and before I move on to the next, think about it!'* Silence can be a very powerful way of communicating.

On a more basic level, pauses are substitutes for punctuation – so you should pause briefly at the end of a sentence. Pauses also allow you to breathe!

The more comfortable you are with silence, the less you will use 'ums' and 'ers' to fill any gaps.

Sit or stand?

This decision depends on your primary aim. A standing position will (generally) exercise more control and authority. Sitting, you invite discussion and participation by being less formal. I would advocate starting 'on your feet' – even if you choose later to sit down, perhaps for questions.

Let's look at how you might use the stage to good effect:

Where to stand
on your 'stage'

Rear of stage		
Flip/screen		Flip/screen
Left	Centre	Right
	Front	

Audience

- the 'front and centre' of the stage should be used at the start and end of your presentation

- the front of your stage should not invade the space of the front row of your audience – it would be intimidating

- step forward (from the centre) to the front of your stage when you want to emphasise a point (what you **must** communicate)

- stepping forward to the front of the stage when you want the audience to participate is effective, providing your body language is more relaxed/inviting. The left and right of the stage front can also be used here

- the centre is where you should spend most of your time but moving from side to side keeps some 'animation' and therefore improves the audience's attention

- the rear of the stage is saying *'I'm not doing anything right now'*. Use it either when you want the attention to be elsewhere – perhaps looking at detailed visuals or when the audience is working on something (at your request) without your involvement

- don't stand between the audience and the visual aids

- remember that as long as you stay 'on-stage' some of the audience will look at you. If you don't want that, leave the stage.

Walk the talk

Your body language should support your words. So if you are seeking to convince the audience on a certain point, adopting hesitant, withdrawn body language will destroy any impact that your words are designed to achieve.

> If the words are a song, your voice the music then your body language is the dance. Those that can perfect the song, music and dance have mastered the art of communicating a message.

There is one golden rule on body language:

> Always be yourself, be natural. Trying to emulate the body language of a speaker you admire will look false.

Body language is a huge topic – it has filled many books in its own right, but here are some key pointers to get you started:

- face your audience – your shoulders (and body) should be parallel to the front row of seats

- avoid any tendency to slouch

- when moving, walk, do not wander – steps should be deliberate

- your feet should be on the ground: don't balance on one leg, don't rock on your heels, don't lean or raise your toes off the floor

- keep your hands away from your neck/head – it is at best distracting and at worst a sign of nervousness

- if you must hold something (for instance, your notes), beware of fidgeting

- use 'open' hand gestures – this means showing the palms, rather than the back of your hands

- if you lose 'control' of your hands (perhaps you start fidgeting), put one hand in a pocket for a little while. I know that others would say this is a definite 'don't do', but it will help you to regain control. However, to retain your composure, ensure that your thumb is outside of the pocket or only your thumb is inside. Do have empty pockets (except, perhaps, for a hankerchief)

- Keep your elbows away from your body – no, don't look like a chicken flapping its wings, just allow the audience to see a small gap between your body and your elbows. It will give you a confident, relaxed appearance

- Body movements should flow – avoid sudden actions. While your body language should not be too over-the-top, it should be somewhat more exaggerated that 'normal'.

Beware that the appropriateness of body language will differ according to the culture of your audience:

> Body language that is acceptable in one culture could be highly offensive in another.

If I itch, do I scratch?

Yes – within reason! Trying to ignore it, will become a distraction to you and potentially cause you to lose track of where you are. If you scratch an itch (briefly), it's gone and your audience will probably not even notice. However, there may be some itches that discretion would say ignore!

Irritating habits you never knew you had

Even now – so far into this book – we still haven't got as far as an actual presentation. Rehearsing your presentation in front of a video camera (or, failing that, a mirror) can reveal all sorts of mannerisms that you never realised you had. For instance:

- Playing with your hair: if you have long hair and tend to flick it away from your eyes, tie your hair back

- subconscious habits – in one video, I heard 'you know' said 26 times in 10 minutes – and I only started counting when it had already started to irritate me!

Eye contact

Look at your audience – especially when making an important point or when challenged by the audience. To do this, you will need to have rehearsed sufficiently so that you won't be looking at your prompts all of the time.

You should seek to make eye contact with as many people in the audience as possible during your presentation. Avoid the natural inclination to make eye contact only with your friends.

Break off eye contact before it becomes a stare.

At the start of your presentation, nerves can intimidate you from making eye contact. If this is how you feel, place your imaginary friend (from the 'being heard' section on page 97) diagonally furthest away from you and look at them. You will, initially, at least, give the impression that you are looking at the audience in front of your 'friend'.

Smiling can be good

Smiling is, in fact, very good – but not if you're announcing to your audience their redundancy!

Smiling says 'I'm glad to be here' (it might even fool the audience!) It encourages the audience to smile and places them more firmly 'on the side' of your presentation and its primary aim.

Rehearsing it as one set piece

Now, you have to put all the elements of presenting together – your appearance, your body language, your voice, your script, your visual aids – everything we have discussed so far in this book. However:

> **If you try to do everything right at the first attempt, it is likely that you will fail on all counts.**

When training or coaching presentation skills, I compare the danger of trying to do too much, too quickly to my somewhat feeble attempt in learning to play the drums:

One Christmas, I was given a drum kit and couldn't master (all at once) the reading of music, the right foot doing one thing and the left another, the left hand playing the snare drum and the right the cymbal (or was it the other way around?). Since I couldn't consciously learn to do everything at once and, being a not-so-patient teenager, I gave up.

Don't fall into this trap. Learn each component part until it becomes a subconscious activity – then move on to the next. So rehearse, rehearse and rehearse again until much of what you do on your 'stage' is subconscious.

When you reach the end of the list of things to learn, go back to the beginning and start again. Never stop learning and refreshing your skills or they won't be there when you really need them.

In summary

- remember that you are a visual aid

- make the first impressions of you gained by the audience count in your favour

- when you are ready to start, walk in a curved line to the front and centre of the stage

- be well-groomed and smart – slightly smarter than your audience

- do not wear new or distracting clothes or jewellery

- project your voice clearly without shouting

- if using a microphone, practice first

- silence that follows an important point is a very powerful way of emphasising it

- make sure you give yourself time to breathe

- sitting down is less formal; standing eases your ability to control events

- deliberate movements around your stage will enliven your presentation

- face your audience, make eye contact and be confident in your body language

- different cultures interpret body language differently. Take care not to innocently (or otherwise) offend your audience

- use rehearsals to identify any irritating habits you may have and try to reduce their frequency

- don't try to apply everything you have learnt at the first attempt; accept that gradual learning through practice is more effective

- smile when you are presenting (unless the message warrants otherwise).

10

Believe it

Everything to do with your presentation must convince the audience to embrace your primary aim. You must create belief.

Believe in your message

If you so much as hint that you do not agree or whole-heartedly support your message, you place the achievement of your primary aim at great risk. And such a hint could be given by:

- an inappropriate word or phrase

- the tone of voice betraying your negative feelings

- a failure in supporting your message with the right body language – for instance, refusing to make eye contact at key points

The tricks to overcome any lack of belief in your message are (short of refusing to do the presentation):

- research the background to the subject to identify why the message needs to be delivered. You may find that once you understand it, you also agree with it

- look for the parts of the message you do believe in and devise a structure to deliver those first – thus reducing the proportion of the message with which you have to be particularly careful

- determine in advance not only the words but also the specific voice and body language you intend to adopt; and rehearse thoroughly.

And if the above still doesn't work:

- write a script about what you do believe (which is contrary to that you will have to deliver). Rehearse this briefly to achieve the right (that is, supportive) voice and body language. Make a powerful presentation by concentrating on everything **except** the words. Then, insert the few words it will take to reverse the message. Rehearse again (now more thoroughly) trying to recreate the same voice and body language you used on your first rehearsal.

Believe in your audience

Welcome your audience. Believe that they want to hear you, believe that they want to get something out of your presentation and this belief will assist you in managing your nerves and negating any fears that you may have.

Seeing your audience as your ally will make it a lot easier than seeing them as an enemy or a group of intimidators.

Believe in yourself

For some, this is perhaps the most difficult of all the beliefs I am asking you to adopt.

Presenters can be scared of losing their way, forgetting what to say, the technology failing or even having a rotten tomato thrown at them!

A few things to remember here:

- if you thoroughly prepare and rehearse, you will minimise the likelihood of forgetting your place

- if you have checked the technology in advance, you will have enough time to sort out any problems

- the likelihood of having anyone throw things at you is minimal – and should it ever happen, providing you handle it calmly, your reputation and that of your presentation can climb sky-high. (No, I am not recommending anyone to adopt the practice).

And, most importantly, remember:

> It is when you are without fear or nerves that you are most likely to make a poor presentation.

Nerves are a good thing

Remember that nerves can be good for you. Yes, they make you work harder, but they will make for a much better presentation. As I said in the introduction – it is when I don't feel nervous, that I'm at my most dangerous!

To help manage your nerves:

- think about the success criteria of your primary aim – assuming that they are reasonable, you will succeed

- before you start, think about how good you will feel when you have finished; think about how good you will feel when you have achieved your primary aim. Think about how good the audience will feel having listened to a great presentation. Remember these good feelings. Go out and present – and enjoy it

- if particularly nervous before you start, consider trying one of the many relaxation techniques available – but don't relax too much!

Believe to be believed

By bringing together the triple beliefs in the message, the audience and yourself, you can and will be believed. There is nothing so powerful in a presenter as one in whom you believe.

> Belief evidences itself by the presenter being credible, trustworthy, positive, enthusiastic and passionate about their subject.

And, if all else fails, remember:

> **Whatever you feel like internally, the trick for success is to exude positive belief externally.**

Conclusion

Prepare, prepare and then prepare

There is no alternative – other than failure – to thorough preparation in delivering a confident presentation.

Having reached this part of the guide (assuming you started at the beginning!), you should realise that there is more to presenting than writing a few words down on paper. So even if you have little time to write, you can still be confident and successful by preparing everything you can in advance. For example:

I mentioned in the opening section of this guide about my father standing for election as a Member of Parliament. During what might be a 3-week campaign, he had to make maybe 100 different speeches to attract as much press coverage as possible. Some were impromptu, some highly organised events. So how did he prepare 100 speeches?

He identified over 50 different points to speak on. These were broad subjects (such as health) or a component part (such as the fate of a local hospital). He then wrote key bullet points about each subject on a separate postcard. Then he wrote three different rather vague introductory postcards and three endings. (Vague to disguise the fact that the middle would vary.)

Having developed a polished delivery style, on arriving to make a speech, he simply took one of the introductory cards, one of the endings and any three for the middle. As a result, every speech was unique – and he got elected!

So even when a presentation could be sprung on you, there is no reason to say that there was no opportunity to prepare.

Rehearse, rehearse and then rehearse

I have also stressed in this guide how important it is to rehearse. Rehearse your presentation style and delivery as much as for an individual presentation.

The purpose of this is not to memorise a script – rather to polish the delivery of the whole event.

Seek feedback from others during a rehearsal to balance the good with the not-so-good. It is too easy to watch oneself on video and say 'I did that wrong, and that, and…'. Remember that the purpose of rehearsing is just as much about saying what's good, what's 'in-the-bag' as what can be improved. When reviewing one's performance alone, these positive advances tend to get overlooked.

Learn for the future

Every presentation, every piece of feedback and every time you see another person presenting is an opportunity to learn. You can learn from presenters that inspire, from those that bore and you can learn from your own experience.

The key is to make that learning a conscious activity and remember it takes time, practice and experience as well as taking advantage of all that you have just read.

This guide has condensed years of practical experience of making presentations – and not just those of the author. Use that experience to make a big step forward in achieving your aims and, ultimately:

> **Enjoy yourself!**